Brad's TEMPER

© 2022 Sierre Johnson
All rights reserved.

ISBN: 979-8-9939896-3-1

Published by Building Bridges 4 Success

Illustrations by Sierre Johnson
Cover design by Sierre Johnson

A Message to our readers

To our readers, families, and supporters,
thank you for believing in stories that build hearts, minds, and brighter futures.
Your love for reading, learning, and emotional growth inspires everything we create.
Every page we share is made with care, purpose, and the hope that it brings comfort, joy, and understanding into your homes.
We are truly grateful for your support and for allowing BBS Books to be a part of your family's story.

With love and appreciation,

BBS the Trio

Brad Jr. is such a nice boy. He is kind and helpful. But sometimes, when things don't go his way, Brad Jr. can become impatient and lose his temper.
One day, Brad Jr. was trying out a new game. It was a tough game and Jr wasn't doing so well at winning.

This made him very, very angry. He began to talk very unkindly to himself. "I am such a loser," he grunted. "I'm no good at this." With every failed attempt, he became more upset. "Grrrrrr!" He growled loudly.

Hearing his negative self talk from the other room, his mommy came to speak to him. "Bradley Jr." she said. "You are not a loser. It's a new game to learn. Be patient and believe in yourself. You can win." His mommy reassured him.

Brad Jr. tried again. And again. But he still did not win. He moaned and groaned, whined and whimpered, flipped and flopped on the bed, and kicked and punched the air in great annoyance with the game.

As he continued to try to win, his little brother and sister, Blake and Sidney, came into his room to play. He ignored them as they jumped around trying to get his attention. He ignored them as they played with his action figures and made them dance with Sidney's dolls. He ignored them as they tried to get him to play hide and seek.

On his fifth try at the game, he lost again. This made him even more angry than before. "Get out of my room!" Brad Jr. yelled angrily. This hurt their feelings. They left his room quietly and sadly.

Brad Jr.'s mom heard what he said to them and she was not happy with his temper.
"Brad Jr.!" She intervened. "Apologize to your brother and sister! That was not kind at all!" She said.

Brad Jr. went to his brother and sister and hugged them. "Blake and Sidney, I apologize," he said calmly and sincerely. "It's this game, it's really getting on my nerves!" He snapped.

"I think you need a time out from the game," his mom said. This made Brad Jr. even more angry. He gritted his teeth, balled his fists tight, and stomped away. His mommy was very unhappy with how angry he was allowing the game to make him. "Come here, right now, Bradley Jr." she snapped. With tears and frustration in his eyes, he returned to his mommy.

Already seeing how angry he was, his mommy decided to hug him instead of speak more about his unpleasant emotions. His mommy knelt down to look him in his eyes. She grabbed his face and kissed his forehead. "Everything is a learning process. We will not be great at everything the first time around. "We have to be patient with ourselves, believe we can learn, and be kind to ourselves when we make mistakes." Mommy said in a very gentle but serious voice.

"I believe in you Brad Jr. you can achieve anything. But you have to believe in yourself too." She said. Brad Jr. understood and hugged his mommy again. Later that evening, after his timeout from the game, his mommy sat with him to learn the game with him. They played the game for a long time and kept losing. But this time, his mommy showed him how to make it a fun learning experience instead of a painful loss.

When they loss, his mommy said "aw man, come on! That's ok! We're not giving up!" Junior was inspired and felt more confident in himself when he didn't allow the game to make him so angry. After a while, his mommy had to go make dinner.

While she was away, Brad Jr. figured out how to win. He tried and tried and tried. On his last attempt, he paused the game, took a deep breath and said "I believe in myself. I am a winner. I can do this." He continued to play the game.

Finally, Brad Jr. won the game. He was so proud of himself for finding his confidence and believing in himself enough to stay calm and see the game through. His mommy and siblings were proud of him, too.

A Note to Caregivers

Frustration and impatience are common emotions for children, especially when they face challenges, setbacks, or unfamiliar tasks. When children struggle, they may express anger toward themselves or others before they understand how to cope with disappointment.

Brad's Temper helps children recognize the impact of negative self-talk, impulsive reactions, and emotional overload. Through patience, guidance, and reassurance, the story models healthy ways to pause, repair mistakes, and build confidence through perseverance.

While reading this story, you may wish to:

- Talk with your child about moments when they feel frustrated or angry

- Identify examples of unkind self-talk and practice replacing it with encouragement

- Practice calming strategies together, such as deep breathing or taking breaks

- Reinforce that mistakes are part of learning and growth

This story reminds children that self-control is learned, not expected overnight, and that love and support remain even when emotions feel big.